NO
STEPS
BEHIND

Beate Sirota Gordon's Battle for Women's Rights in Japan

By Jeff Gottesfeld
Illustrated by Shiella Witanto

Creston Books

女は三歩下がって歩く

Onna-wa san-po sagatte aruku.

Women walk three steps behind.

— Old Japanese proverb

On a gray day in 1929, a young Jewish girl named Beate stood wide-eyed at the rail of an enormous steamship as it eased into Yokohama harbor. Her father, Leo Sirota, was a famous pianist who had left anti-Semitic Russia for opportunity in Austria. His talent brought the family to Japan. When they arrived, Beate had never before seen an Asian person.

The girl had an ear for languages. She learned fluent Japanese and came to love her new home. Sunrise from the crest of Nogi Hill. The beautiful words for thank you: dōmo arigatō. Hanetsuki badminton and kanji drawing with her best friend Akara. The boom of taiko drums and the rustle of her yukata in the moonlight.

She also discovered Japan's unfair side. There was a small movement for women's rights, but men still controlled everything. Fathers could sell daughters to strangers. In the bustling Ginza market, some wives walked three steps behind their husbands. At many gatherings, women had no place at the table. Even Akara looked at the floor if a strange man entered the room.

Ugly proverbs made Beate bristle.

女の知恵は鼻の先

Onna-no chie-wa
hana-no saki

*The wisdom of
women is at the
end of the nose.*

女の情に蛇が住む

Onna-no nasake-ni
hebi-ga sumu

*In women's hearts
dwell serpents.*

女は魔物

Onna-wa mamono

Women are devilish.

As Beate grew older, the world grew hateful. Adolph Hitler led Nazi Germany to war and the "Final Solution" to rid the world of Jews. Japan allied with Germany and invaded China, where its soldiers slaughtered millions.

When Beate was 15 and ready for college, few girls were allowed in Japanese universities and return to Europe was out of the question. Her parents sent her where they thought she could be safe -- Mills College in Oakland, California, an American school especially for women. There they learned to be doctors, scientists, artists, and writers.

The very first day, the college president gave a speech about equal rights.

Beate had never heard anything like it.

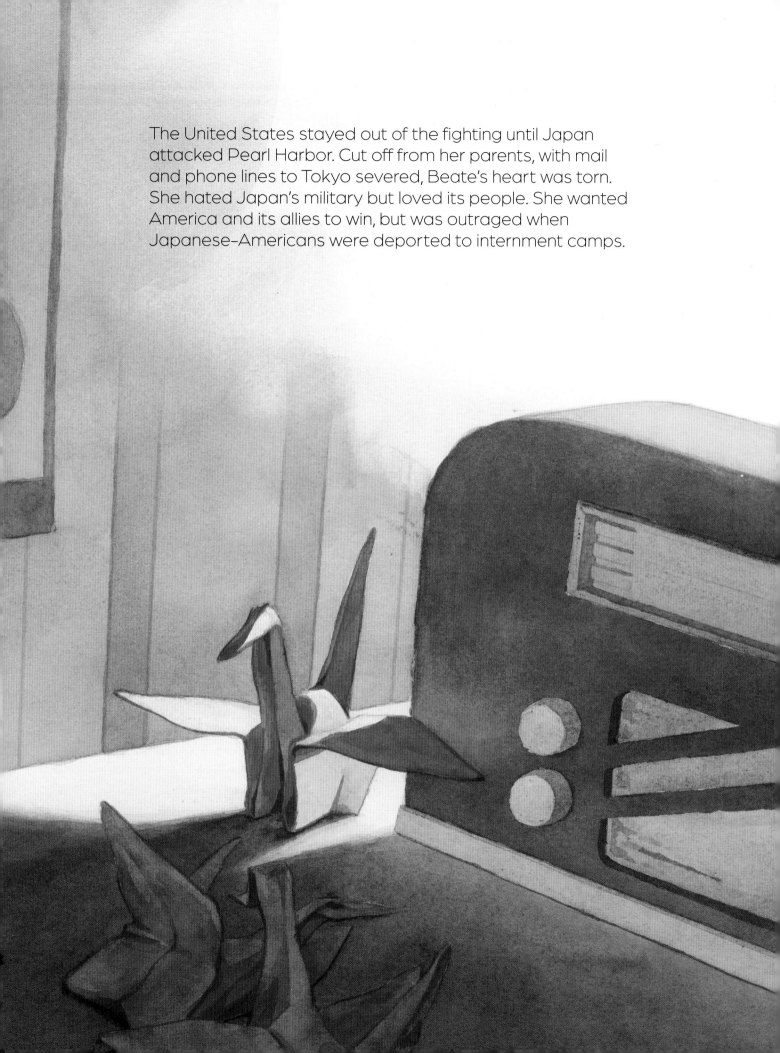

The United States stayed out of the fighting until Japan attacked Pearl Harbor. Cut off from her parents, with mail and phone lines to Tokyo severed, Beate's heart was torn. She hated Japan's military but loved its people. She wanted America and its allies to win, but was outraged when Japanese-Americans were deported to internment camps.

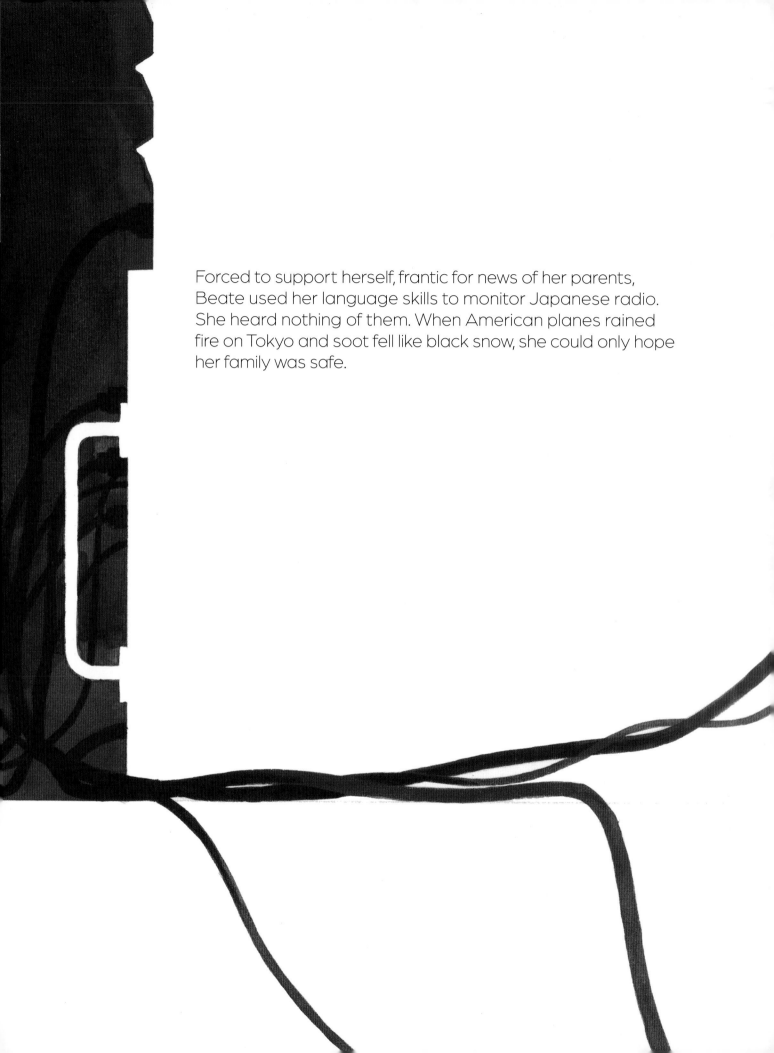

Forced to support herself, frantic for news of her parents, Beate used her language skills to monitor Japanese radio. She heard nothing of them. When American planes rained fire on Tokyo and soot fell like black snow, she could only hope her family was safe.

A joyless August morning saw the atomic attack on Hiroshima, but Japan's surrender still brought no word from her parents. With travel there forbidden to civilians, Beate begged the Army for a job. Rebuilding a country didn't seem like women's work to them, but when they heard her perfect Japanese, they hired her as a researcher and an interpreter.

Aboard a crowded troop plane, Beate got her first glimpse of Japan in years. Her face was as ashen as her beloved country.

Once on the ground, Beate searched desperately for her mother and father. The Ginza was flattened. At her family's house, a single charred pillar teetered in the wreckage.

But that night, she heard a faint, familiar voice in the hotel lobby:

"Beate!"

It was her father. He had learned of her arrival. Thin as piano wire, he explained that her mother was freezing in a remote mountain cabin. Japan had interned all foreigners. Beate and her father rushed there with Army-issue chocolate bars. Finally reunited, the family drank glassful after glassful of steaming tea heated on a tiny stove.

With her parents safe, Beate got to work. General MacArthur was in charge of the Occupation. When his team discovered how well the young translator knew the country, they assigned her to help write Japan's new Constitution — the nation's basic law.

Beate was just 22, the only woman in a room of lawyers and officers. She asked herself, "What do I know about constitutions?" Determined to learn, she scoured Tokyo for useful books. A few libraries had survived, battered guardians of hope to help people turn from war to peace.

The general wanted Japan to have an elected government. Beate knew that even with elections, men would seize power. Japan would remain a place where fathers sold daughters like fish at the market, girls were forced to marry, and women walked three steps behind.

The only one who could speak for Japan's women was Beate. She drafted a long list of changes to ensure their place at the table of the future and brought her ideas to her commanding officer.

He protested. "You have given Japanese women more rights than are in the American Constitution!"

Beate responded calmly. "Colonel Kades, that's not very difficult to do, because women are not in the American Constitution." She was so stubborn and persuasive that the colonel finally agreed to her biggest demands. Beate wrote the words herself.

第十四条　すべて国民は、法の下に平等であつて、人種、信条、性別、社会的身分又は門地により、政治的、経済的又は社会的関係において、差別されない

All of the people are equal under the law and there shall be no discrimination in political, economic or social relations because of race, creed, sex, social status or family origin.

— From Article 14, Japanese constitution

Home Minister Matsumoto led a delegation to discuss the proposed new law. Again, Beate was the only woman at the table. The Japanese delegates admired her perfect diction and swift translations. They called her Beate-san and told her dōmo arigatō. But when the Americans proposed Article 14, the delegation was furious. Beate fumed, but reported their words precisely:

"This doesn't fit our culture, doesn't fit our history, doesn't fit our way of life!"

Debate raged for hours. Finally, Colonel Kades spoke. "This article was written by Miss Sirota herself. She has her heart set on this issue. Why don't we just pass it?"

The delegates stared. Beate-san wrote this? This young woman raised in their country, who knew their customs and spoke like a native? The woman they respected so much?

Beate fixed her eyes on them. Not on the floor.

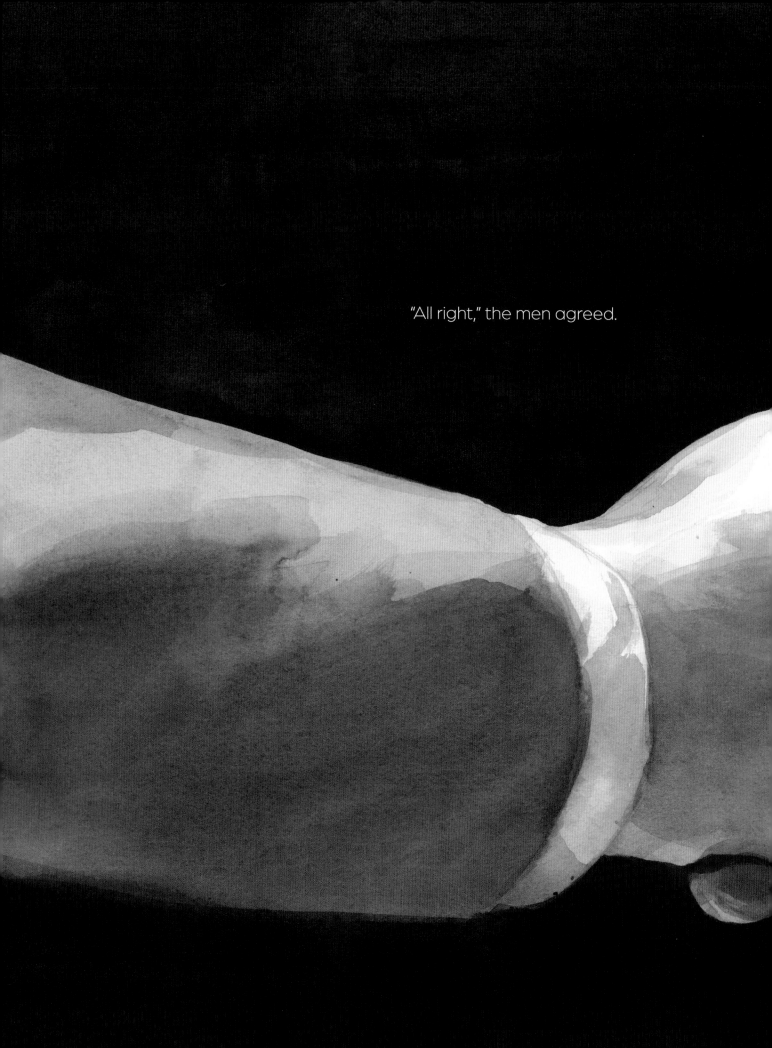

"All right," the men agreed.

"We'll do it your way."

The story should have made headlines:
a young woman had changed a nation's
future. But the United States considered
it a security secret.

Decades later, when she was finally permitted to talk of what she'd done, Beate returned to Tokyo.

She discovered she was a hero.

There were speeches and concerts in her honor. The government gave her a special award. Her reunion with her childhood friend Akara, now a professor of French, was national news.

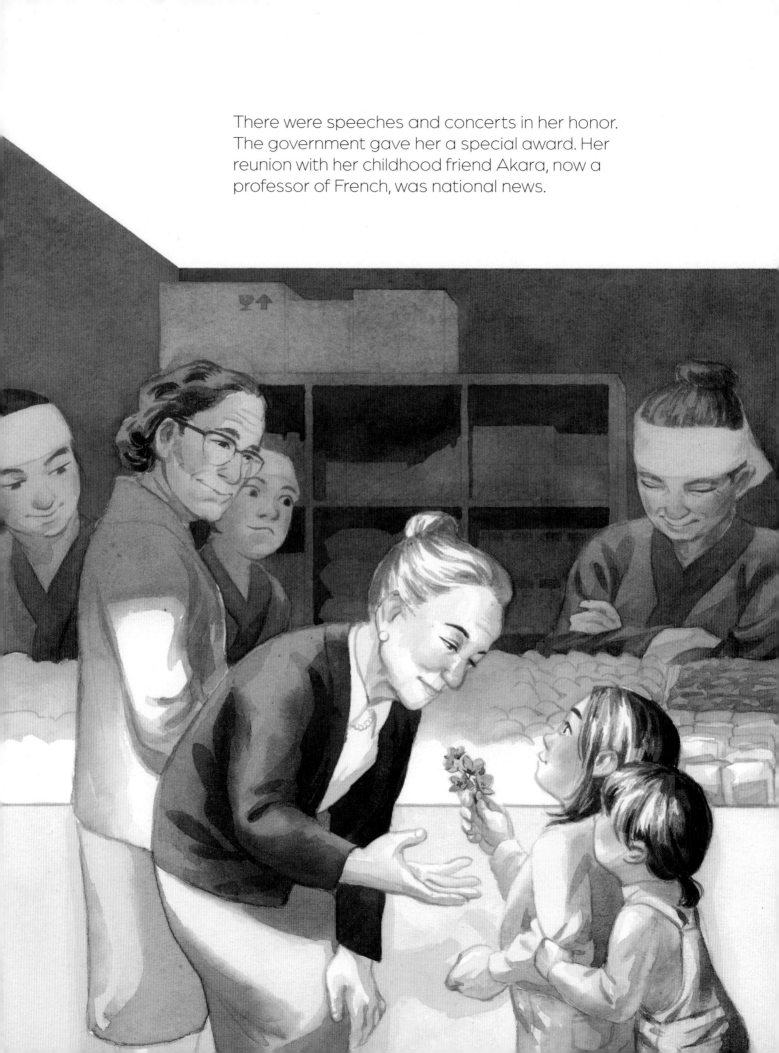

Women were doctors, scientists, artists, and writers. In the Ginza, no woman walked three steps behind. Instead, they rushed to greet her.

"Dōmo arigatō, Beate-san! Dōmo arigatō!"

As they embraced, Beate may well have recalled another old proverb:

Onna nara–dewa yo–ga akenu

Without women, the dawn doesn't break.

女ならでは夜が明けぬ

Author's Note

Beate (Bee-AH-tay) Sirota Gordon was born in Vienna in 1923. Her father was Leo Sirota, a world-famous pianist who left anti-Semitic Russia for opportunity in Austria. When the economy collapsed in the late 1920s and concert halls were shuttered, Sirota accepted a teaching position in Japan that would also give him a place to perform. Beate made many friends in Tokyo, among them Akara Umehara, daughter of the famed Japanese painter Ryūzaburō Umehara. The decision to go to Japan likely saved the Sirota family, as the anti-Semitism which swept through Germany and Austria ultimately led to the Holocaust. That's why, when it came time for Beate to attend college, a return to Europe was impossible. The Nazis had stripped her of her citizenship. It was dangerous for Jews to live there. They were fleeing Germany and Austria, not returning.

Though Japan mistreated its Jews, it did not slaughter them as their Nazis allies wanted, not even in the areas it occupied. However, the Japanese military's reign of terror in much of south Asia resulted in millions of innocent civilians being killed, kidnapped, and enslaved. Women, children, and babies suffered particularly horrifying fates. As for the U.S., historians and ethicists are fiercely split on President Harry Truman's decision to use atomic weapons on Hiroshima and Nagasaki, where hundreds of thousands of Japanese civilians died from the blasts and radiation. The firebombing of Tokyo on the night of March 9-10, 1945 – known in Japan then as the Night of Black Snow – is less well known, but took nearly as large a toll as either atomic attack. The Supreme Court only recently admitted — in June, 2018 — that the Japanese-American internments were unconstitutional. Nearly 120,000 people of Japanese descent were imprisoned in bleak camps, forced to sell their homes and businesses or leave them in the care of neighbors and associates. The U.S. government still hasn't paid meaningful reparations for the losses incurred by these families, though a token amount was granted decades later in 1988.

Beate's contributions to the Japanese constitution are enshrined in articles 14 and 24:

Article 14:

1. All of the people are equal under the law and there shall be no discrimination in political, economic or social relations because of race, creed, sex, social status or family origin.

Article 24:

1. Marriage shall be based only on the mutual consent of both sexes and it shall be maintained through mutual cooperation with the equal rights of husband and wife as a basis.

2. With regard to choice of spouse, property rights, inheritance, choice of domicile, divorce and other matters pertaining to marriage and the family, laws shall be enacted from the standpoint of individual dignity and the essential equality of the sexes.

Beate prepared other language, guaranteeing health care for families and abolishing child labor, but the American delegation refused to suggest such radical ideas to their Japanese counterparts.

It is important to note that in the first decades of the 20th century, there was a fledgling movement among Japanese women calling for participation in political discourse, the right to vote, and better representation in society. This movement was inspired by the late 19th century feminist Toshiko Kishida and led by such

Beate in Japan, 1946

luminaries as Fusae Ichikawa. Representatives of that movement were not offered a place at the table, neither by the Japanese nor the Americans, when the post-war constitution was negotiated.

When Beate returned to America in 1947, she married Joseph Gordon, another Jewish translator, who had been Chief of the Interpreters' Section in Tokyo. They settled in New York City and had two children. Her parents came to New York City as well. Later, she was instrumental in creating post-war harmony between the United States and Japan as a cultural programmer and leader of the Asia Society. Like so much having to do with national security, the story of the post-war constitution, and Beate's pivotal role in its creation, remained a military secret for decades. Beate gave no interviews to the Japanese press until the 1990s. When she finally returned to Japan, the Japanese government awarded her the Order of the Sacred Treasure, Gold Rays with Rosette. She became the subject of hundreds of articles, documentaries, films, books, and plays, and remains a Japanese national hero. Her memoir, *The Only Woman in the Room*, was published in Japanese before it was translated to English. The title inspired some words in this book.

Beate died on December 30, 2012. Her children scattered her ashes in Japan.

As of the writing of this book, despite many attempts to pass such an amendment, the Constitution of the United States of America still does not guarantee equal rights for women.

America also has far to go in the treatment of immigrants. Shiella Witanto, this book's illustrator, came to the United States legally in 2012 from Indonesia, to study at the Academy of Art University in San Francisco, California. She quickly became a sought-after illustrator and was granted permanent residency. Soon after she completed the art for *No Steps Behind*, her Green Card renewal was denied. Shiella had two weeks to pack up and return to Indonesia or face deportation. She is there now.

References

Beate discusses her reunion in Tokyo with her father and his calling of her name, "Beate!" in her memoir, *The Only Woman in the Room,* page 16.

"What do I know about constitutions?" The quote comes from an interview that Beate did with WGBH public radio in Boston, on the show "Morning Streams," on November 11, 2005 (http://streams.wgbh.org/online/morn/transcripts/MSPC20051111.pdf).

"Colonel Kades, that's not very difficult to do, because women are not in the American Constitution." The conversation between Colonel Kades and Beate is documented in two places. First, it is recounted in an article in the May 28, 2005 edition of the *New York Times,* about a visit by Beate to Japan in 2005 (http://www.nytimes.com/2005/05/28/world/asia/fighting-to-protect-her-gift-to-japanese-women.html). Second, Beate recounts in her memoir (page 116) how in the grueling week of debate, almost all of the clauses that emerged from her Underwood typewriter ended up in the trash basket.

The sequence that runs from the Japanese negotiators stating, "This doesn't fit our culture, doesn't fit our history, doesn't fit our way of life!" through Colonel Kates declaring, "This article was written by Miss Sirota herself. She has her heart set on this issue. Why don't we just pass it?" to the Japanese delegation acceding, "All right," the men agreed. "We'll do it your way," comes from two sources. The opening line is quoted in the Jewish Women's Archive (https://jwa.org/thisweek/oct/25/1923/birth-of-beate-sirota-gordon-who-wrote-equality-into-post-war-japanese), while Beate writes about the rest of the encounter in her memoir *The Only Woman in the Room* (page 123 ff).

"Dōmo arigatō, Beate-san! Dōmo arigatō!" This came from an interview with Nicole Gordon, Beate's daughter, on May 8, 2013. It is confirmed by an interview that Beate did with the ABC network show "Nightline" on Wednesday, February 10, 1999, where she told host Ted Koppel, "They always want their picture taken with me. They always want to shake my hand. They always tell me how grateful they are. I'm always on a high when I'm in Japan. I'm surrounded by so much love and it's really inspiring." (https://www2.kenyon.edu/Depts/Religion/Fac/Adler/Reln275/Sirota.htm)

In this text, the western convention of first-name followed by family name is followed for the sake of simplicity. Kanji, translation, and transliterations were verified by Prof. Hideko Abe. The hyphenated transliteration style is to help young readers with pronunciation.

Beate with Fusae Ichikawa at The League of Women Voters, 1952

Bibliographic Notes

Beate's life is extraordinarily well documented in Japanese, but not as much in English. The starting place to learn more is Beate's 1997 memoir, *The Only Woman in the Room: A Memoir of Japan, Human Rights, and the Arts,* published by Kodansha, with a later edition from the University of Chicago Press. Another biography of Beate is Nazrine Azzimi and Michel Wasserman's *Last Boat to Yokohama,* published in 2015 by Three Rooms Press.

Beate participated in a number of extensive oral histories for various archives. The one most helpful to me was with the Columbia University Center for Oral History, conducted by Aaron Skaebelund and Nicole Cohen beginning on 15 October 2001. There are other oral histories, such as the ones at the University of Maryland (http://lib.guides.umd.edu/c.php?g=326790&p=2194124) and at the Imperial War Museum in London, UK (https://www.iwm.org.uk/collections/item/object/80022530). Mills College opened access to her personal archive in late April, 2019.

There are many newspaper, magazine, and other journalistic (both in print and online) references to Beate's life. Among the most helpful are the *New York Times* obituary (https://www.nytimes.com/2013/01/02/world/asia/beate-gordon-feminist-heroine-in-japan-dies-at-89.html), the obituary in *The Economist* (https://www.economist.com/obituary/2013/01/12/beate-gordon), the obituary in *The Atlantic* (https://www.theatlantic.com/sexes/archive/2013/01/the-american-woman-who-wrote-equal-rights-into-japans-constitution/266856/), and the *Japan Times* review of her memoir (https://www.economist.com/obituary/2013/01/12/beate-gordon). A *Jewish Women's Archive* piece on Beate (https://jwa.org/blog/meet-beate-sirota-gordon-who-knew) and the obituary in *The Forward* (https://forward.com/news/168592/beate-sirota-gordon-dies-at-89/) both help to assess her life in a Jewish context. For those interested in photographs, *The Forward* offers a link to a large archive that is in the public domain.

Video footage of Beate is extensive. She speaks for more than an hour in this appearance at Middlebury College (Vermont) in 2007 (https://www.youtube.com/watch?v=TceZiTqyZXI), and was the commencement speaker at Mills College in 2011 (https://www.youtube.com/watch?v=O6GIcAlJeZ8) . Beate speaks Japanese in this appearance on Japanese television (https://www.youtube.com/watch?v=qTOixvhaGzk) and in this 2012 small feature story (https://www.youtube.com/watch?v=nbQ0BZwNVWg).

Special Thanks To....

Nicole Gordon (daughter of Beate Sirota Gordon), Hiroko Shimada-Watanabe (granddaughter of Akara Umehara), Misa Sugiura, Jeremy Blaustein, Cynthia Kadohata, Akiko White, Patricia Graham, DeAnn Okamura, and Yoshio Nakamaru (translator). Enormous gratitude to Prof. Hideko Abe, chair of the East Asian Studies department at Colby College, where I graduated a very long time ago, Akari Shibata, former Japanese instructor at Colby, David Jacobson for magnificent fact-checking, and Dr. Beth Leedham. My editor and publisher Marissa Moss cared as much about this book as I do. My agent and friend Laura Blake Peterson was, is, and always will be the best ally any author could want.

Timeline

1885, May 4	Leo Sirota, born in Kiev, Ukraine (controlled by Russia)
1893, July 28	Augustine Horenstein born, Vienna, Austria.
1903 to 1905	Pogroms against the Jews sweep through the Russian empire, in scores of communities, including Kishinev, Odessa, Melitopol, Yekaterinoslav, Romny, and Kiev.
1904, Autumn	Leo moves to Vienna, Austria to escape the violence.
1920	Leo and Augustine marry in Vienna, Austria.
1923, October 25	Beate born in Vienna, Austria.
1921 to 1928	In aftermath of World War I, Austria struggles economically, first with hyperinflation, then with slow growth.
1929, Summer	Sirota family travels to Tokyo. The voyage takes weeks.
1933, January	Adolf Hitler comes to power in Germany and introduces the new anti-Jewish laws, precursors to the Nazi plan to exterminate all Jews.
1937, July	Japan invades China, civilian massacres begin.
1938, March	Nazi Germany annexes Austria; Jews stripped of citizenship. Sirotas are now stateless.
1939	Beate graduates high school, goes to Oakland, California to attend Mills College.
1940, September	Japan, Germany, and Italy form the "Axis" alliance.
1941, December 7	Japanese attack on Pearl Harbor, Hawaii. America declares war on Japan and Germany. All contact between the people in Japan and those in the United States is cut off. Beate cannot write to her parents, and they cannot write to her.
1942, Feburary 19	President Roosevelt issues Executive Order 9066, for internment of Japanese-Americans in isolated camps.
1942	Beate translates Japanese radio broadcasts in San Francisco to support herself.
1943	Beate graduates from Mills College and then finds work with Office of War Information.
1945, January	Beate becomes an American citizen.
1945, March	American planes firebomb Tokyo. Other Japanese cities also attacked.
1945, August 6	American atomic attack on Hiroshima. Nagasaki similarly bombed on August 9.
1945, August 15	Japan surrenders to America but remains a closed military zone.
1945, Autumn	Beate hired by the United States Foreign Economic Administration. She convinces the U.S. Army to use her as an interpreter in Japan.
1945, Christmas Eve	Beate returns to Tokyo.
1945, Christmas Day	Beate reunites with her father, and soon afterward, her mother.
1946, February 4	Beate assigned to work on new post-war constitution draft, due in a week.
1946, February 4-10	Beate's two human rights clauses accepted by her superior officers.
1946, March 4-5	All-day/night meeting where Beate's clauses are accepted by the Japanese.
1946, May 22	Still stateless, Leo and Augustine Sirota admitted to United States as parents of a citizen.
1947, May 3	New Japanese constitution becomes law.
1947, June	Beate returns to New York City.
1998	Beate honored by Japanese government with Order of the Sacred Treasure, Gold Rays with Rosette.
2012, December 30	Beate dies in New York City. Hundreds of articles about her in Japanese press.
2019, April	Beate's personal archive opens at Mills College.

About the Authors

Jeff Gottesfeld is an acclaimed writer for page, stage, and screen. His work has won awards from the American Library Association, Association of Jewish Libraries, International Reading Association, Writer's Guild of America, and the National Council for the Social Studies, and been translated into many languages. He lives in Los Angeles. Visit him at jeffgottesfeldwriter.com

Shiella Witanto draws or paints all day long. She grew up in Indonesia, where her hometown of Bandung has the best bowl of chicken noodles in the world. She studied illustration at the Academy of Art University in San Francisco. *No Steps Behind* is her first book. After six years in the United States she was forced to return to Indonesia due to new immigration policies. She now lives in Jawa Barat, Indonesia and continues to make art everyday. You can see her illustrations and read more about her at shiellawitanto.com.

More Praise for
No Steps Behind:

"Beate Sirota's timeless story reveals the power of education to transform lives and countries both. Mills couldn't be prouder of her!"
— Elizabeth Hillman, President, Mills College

"A stunning biographical picture book that will expand your understanding of Japan, its history, and its conflicts."
— Viki Radford, Librarian, Yokohama International School

"There's a lot of work and passion in this book."
– Yuko Shimizu, best-selling illustrator of *Barbed Wire Baseball*, winner of the California Young Reader Award.